# CIRCULATION

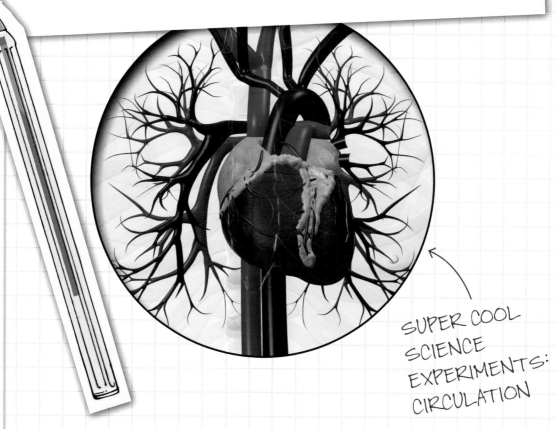

SUPER COOL
SCIENCE
EXPERIMENTS:
CIRCULATION

by Tamra B. Orr

CHERRY LAKE PUBLISHING • ANN ARBOR, MICHIGAN

CHERRY LAKE Publishing

A NOTE TO PARENTS AND TEACHERS: Please review the instructions for these experiments before your children do them. Be sure to help them with any experiments you do not think they can safely conduct on their own.

A NOTE TO KIDS: Be sure to ask an adult for help with these experiments when you need it. Always put your safety first!

Published in the United States of America by
Cherry Lake Publishing
Ann Arbor, Michigan
www.cherrylakepublishing.com

Content Editor: Robert Wolffe, EdD,
Professor of Teacher Education,
Bradley University, Peoria, Illinois

Book design and illustration: The Design Lab

Photo Credits: Cover and page 1, ©Sebastian Kaulitzki, used under
license from Shutterstock, Inc.; page 5, ©Chamillewhite/Dreamstime.
com; page 9, ©Sebastian Kaulitzki/Alamy; page 13, ©Redchopsticks.com
LLC/Alamy; page 18, ©iStockphoto.com/jgroup; page 22, ©artpartner-
images.com/Alamy; page 26, ©Iofoto/Dreamstime.com

Library of Congress Cataloging-in-Publication Data
Orr, Tamra.
   Super cool science experiments: Circulation / by Tamra B. Orr.
       p. cm.—(Science explorer)
   Includes bibliographical references and index.
   ISBN-13: 978-1-60279-520-4        ISBN-10: 1-60279-520-7 (lib. bdg.)
   ISBN-13: 978-1-60279-599-0        ISBN-10: 1-60279-599-1 (pbk.)
   1. Cardiovascular system—Juvenile literature. I. Title. II. Title:
Circulation. III. Series.
   QP103.O77 2010
   612.1—dc22                              2009004309

Cherry Lake Publishing would like to acknowledge the work
of The Partnership for 21st Century Skills. Please visit
www.21stcenturyskills.org for more information.

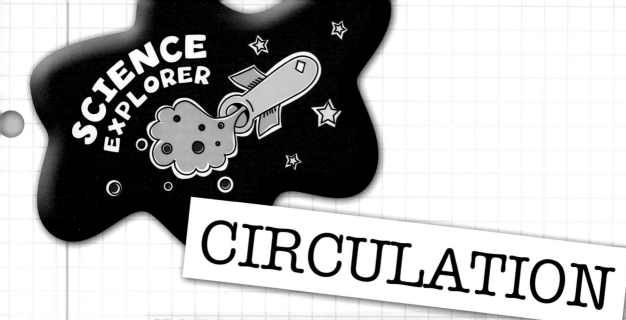

# CIRCULATION

## TABLE OF CONTENTS

# The Science under Your Skin

Your body is a complicated machine. It is made up of many different parts. When these different parts work together, they are called systems. One important system in your body is called the circulatory system. It includes your heart and all of your blood vessels. All of the blood in your body moves through the circulatory system. You have many amazing, scientific things just under your skin!

Scientists and doctors study the body's different systems to learn how they work. Scientists perform experiments to test their ideas about the body. In this book, we'll study the circulatory system. We'll do experiments with circulation, and we'll learn to think like scientists.

# First Things First

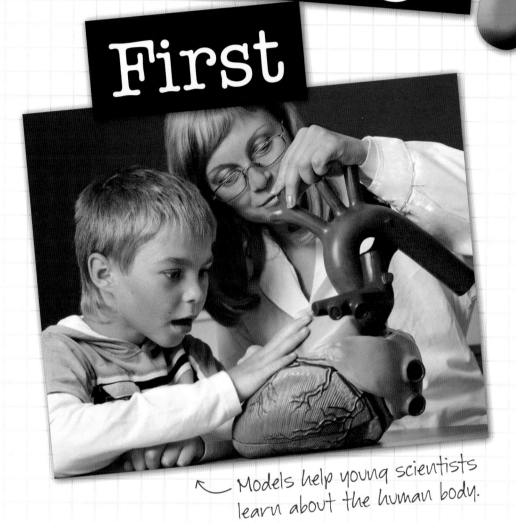

← Models help young scientists learn about the human body.

Scientists learn by studying nature very carefully. For example, scientists who study the human body watch to see how things work and what happens if something goes wrong. They use their observations to make logical guesses about nature and do experiments to test those guesses.

When scientists design experiments, they must think very clearly. The way they think about problems is often called the scientific method. What is the scientific method? It's a step-by-step way of finding answers to specific questions. The steps don't always follow the same pattern. Sometimes scientists change their minds. The process often works something like this:

*Scientific method*

- **Step One:** A scientist gathers the facts and makes observations about one particular thing.
- **Step Two:** The scientist comes up with a question that is not answered by all the observations and facts.
- **Step Three:** The scientist creates a hypothesis. This is a statement of what the scientist thinks is probably the answer to the question.
- **Step Four:** The scientist tests the hypothesis. He or she designs an experiment to see whether the hypothesis is correct. The scientist does the experiment and writes down what happens.
- **Step Five:** The scientist draws a conclusion based on how the experiment turned out. The conclusion might be that the hypothesis is correct. Sometimes, though, the hypothesis is not correct. In that case, the scientist might develop a new hypothesis and another experiment.

In the following experiments, we'll see the scientific method in action. We'll gather some facts and observations about circulation. And for each experiment, we'll develop a question and a hypothesis. Next, we'll do an actual experiment to see if our hypothesis is correct. By the end of the experiment, we should know something new about the human body. Scientists, are you ready? Let's get started!

Don't forget to write down what happens when you do your experiments.

7

# Experiment #1

## The Mighty Muscle

Have you ever looked at your muscles in the mirror? You might have flexed your arm to see your bicep muscles or stood on tiptoe to see the muscles in your calf. These muscles are strong. One of your strongest muscles, however, is one you can't see. It is your heart! Even though it is only about the size of your fist, it is mighty.

Think about it. Your heart never stops. Try holding a rubber ball and squeezing it in your hand over and over. How many times can you squeeze it before your arm gets tired? Your arm muscles are strong, but they need to rest. Your heart doesn't. Even when you are sleeping, it keeps right on working. It beats 100,000 times a day. That's 40 million times a year. Over your lifetime, your heart beats at least 2 billion times! Just like any other healthy muscle, the more you use it, the stronger it gets.

Your heart is extremely important. It pumps blood throughout your body and back to your heart again. The blood travels around your body through a system of tubes called blood vessels. Blood vessels include arteries, veins, and capillaries. This is known as your circulatory system, because

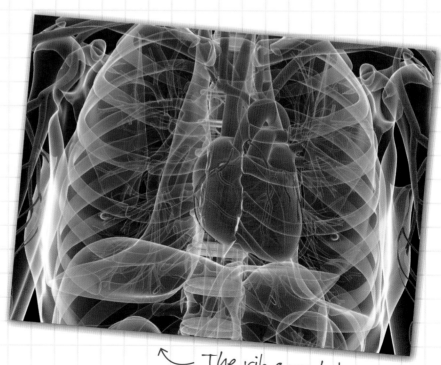

The rib cage helps protect the heart.

blood circulates from your heart to the different parts of your body and then back to the heart. As the blood travels, it brings oxygen to each cell in your body. Then the circulatory system brings the blood back to your heart.

The heart is made of four chambers called the left and right atria and the left and right ventricles. The atria collect blood as it returns to the heart. Then they send the blood to the ventricles. The ventricles pump the blood back out again. Over the course of a single day, 10 pints of blood go through your entire circulatory system 1,000 times.

Your heart also has valves. Valves are like little doors. As your heart pumps blood in and out, the valves make a noise that sounds like *lub-dub, lub-dub*. This is usually called your heartbeat. Doctors use a stethoscope to listen to it. This tool makes the sound easier to hear. Let's build our own stethoscope and do our first experiment. Let's test our own hearts!

How many times does your heart beat per minute? For kids, the average is between 90 and 120 beats per minute. Different activities can make your heart speed up or slow down. What do you think happens to your heartbeat when you exercise? Let's form a hypothesis that answers this question: **When people are active or excited, their hearts beat faster.** Now, let's test your hypothesis.

**Here's what you'll need:**
- A cardboard tube from a paper towel roll
- An assistant
- A watch or timer
- A pencil and paper

Experiments are more fun when you do them with a friend.

**Instructions:**

1. Place one end of the cardboard tube against your assistant's chest. Place the other end to your ear. Can you hear the heart beating? If not, adjust the tube until the sound is clear.

Lub-dub,
lub-dub,
lub-dub . . .

2. While your assistant is sitting down, count how many times his or her heart beats in 1 minute. As you count the beats, be sure to keep an eye on the time. Stop counting after 1 minute has passed. Write down the number.

3. Have your assistant stand up and run in place for 30 seconds. Then listen to his or her heartbeat again. Is it different? How many times did it beat after exercise? Write down that number.

Your heart muscles have to be tough. They pump blood through your body all day, every day without ever stopping. In fact, your heart muscles work twice as hard as your leg muscles when you are running a race.

**Conclusion:**

What conclusion can you make about how exercise might affect your heart? Was your hypothesis correct?

# Experiment #2 Feel the Beat

↖ Your pulse beats in time with your heart.

Has a doctor ever checked your pulse? Your pulse is a throbbing feeling made by the blood passing through your arteries. When the doctor checked your pulse, he or she might have held your wrist or put his or her hand on your neck. Have you wondered exactly what the doctor was doing? Let's find out.

The only way that your heart can get blood to your entire body is through your arteries. Arteries are large tubes that carry blood from the heart to the rest of the body. Veins are smaller tubes that take blood back to the heart. Capillaries are even smaller tubes that carry blood between cells. You have a lot of blood vessels! In fact, if you could line them up end to end, they would stretch out more than 60,000 miles (96,560 kilometers).

These tubes come in all sizes. The largest one of all is your aorta. It is an artery as big around as a garden hose. It supplies blood to the heart muscle, head, arms, legs, chest, stomach, kidneys, intestines, and other organs. The smallest tubes in your body are called capillaries. Capillaries are very tiny. In fact, they are 10 times thinner than a human hair!

There are two areas where it is easiest to feel your pulse. The first is on the inside of your wrist, just below your thumb. This is called your radial pulse. The other is on both sides of your neck, near the front. This is called your carotid pulse. You should only check one side of your neck at a time.

As blood flows through your arteries, they expand and contract with each heartbeat. As you move around, your pulse gets faster—you found that out in the first experiment. What else can affect your pulse? Let's state a hypothesis: **Your pulse can speed up or slow down for reasons other than being more or less active.** Let's perform an experiment to test it.

## Here's what you'll need:

- A watch or timer that can measure seconds
- A friend
- Different types of recorded music (and something to play them on)
- A pencil and paper
- A good imagination

Make sure the music isn't too loud. You don't want to hurt your ears!

## Instructions:

1. Use your pointer and middle fingers to find the pulse in your neck. You can do this by pressing the tips of these fingers firmly against the skin on the side of your neck. Then move them across your neck until you find your pulse. Your pulse feels like a thumping under your fingertips.
2. Once you have found your pulse, count the beats for 15 seconds, keeping an eye on your watch. Multiply that number by 4 to figure out how many times your heart is beating per minute.

3. Have your friend put on some very loud, very powerful music. Wait a few seconds, and then check your heart rate again. Write down your observations. When the song is over, check your pulse again. Did your heart rate go up or down?

4. Now, have your friend put on some quiet, calm music. Wait a few seconds, and check your pulse. Write it down. Do the same thing at the end of the song.

5. Now, it's time to use your imagination. Close your eyes and take a few deep breaths. Think about something that you like to do. It might be riding your bike on a summer day or watching a movie with your friends. It could be hanging out with your family or spending time reading in your room. It should feel relaxing and comfortable. Now, check your pulse and write it down.

Relax and imagine doing something fun!

6. Imagine doing something scary. It might be facing a hard test, riding a roller coaster, or being in trouble with the principal. It should be threatening, and your breathing should speed up. What happens to your heart rate now?

**Conclusion:**

With this experiment, you have discovered that your heartbeat can also be changed by things such as what kind of music you listen to or what you are thinking about at the moment. How much did it change? What else can you think of to test? Try checking before and after playing a video game or watching an action-packed movie. What do you think you will find out?

Your blood circulates through your entire body between 1 and 3 times a minute! This means that, in 1 day, it travels a total of 12,000 miles (19,312 km). That is like traveling from New York City to Los Angeles 4 times in 1 day!

# Experiment #3

## An Amazing Trip

← Blood cells look red when they are carrying oxygen.

As amazing as the heart muscle is, it would not work if it were not connected to veins and arteries. The veins, arteries, and capillaries are like highways, streets, and avenues. The blood uses these roads to travel to where it needs to go in the body. It also uses these roads to travel back to the heart. Blood travels quickly through the body.

It carries oxygen, chemicals, and fuel to the body's cells through arteries. Then it takes away waste products through the veins.

How do these tubes work? The heart pumps blood through the arteries. Blood moves through veins from the push of the muscles around the veins. What about those tiny capillaries? There the blood moves through osmosis. Osmosis is a process of absorption, in which materials move through partly solid walls, like the walls of a capillary. How does this work? Do you think that water could move through something as hard as a piece of potato? Here are two possible hypotheses to choose from:

**Hypothesis #1: Water can move through a piece of potato.**

**Hypothesis #2: Water cannot move through a piece of potato.**

Now let's do an experiment to test your hypothesis.

**Here's what you'll need:**
- 2 bowls
- Water
- A sharp knife
- A potato
- 2 tablespoons of salt
- An adult helper

## Instructions:

1. Fill both of the bowls with several inches of water.
2. Have an adult slice your potato lengthwise into 8 pieces. Make sure that each piece has 2 flat sides.
3. Add the salt to 1 of the bowls.
4. Put 4 potato pieces in the bowl with salted water. Put the other 4 potato pieces in the bowl with the plain water.
5. Let the potatoes soak for 20 minutes. Then look at the potatoes. Can you see a difference between the 2 sets of potatoes?

What do you think is going to happen to the potatoes?

**Conclusion:**

The potatoes in the bowl with salt water were limp and kind of floppy. The potato pieces in the bowl with plain water were firm. Why? Water tends to move across membranes from areas of lower salt concentration to areas with a higher salt concentration. When you added salt to the water in one bowl, you increased the concentration of salt. So water moved out of the potato into the bowl. Was your hypothesis correct? Did you correctly predict the results of this experiment?

Blood is made up of many elements. A single drop of blood contains 5 million red blood cells. Red blood cells carry oxygen. They also carry carbon dioxide. Carbon dioxide is the waste gas that cells produce. Blood cells carry carbon dioxide back to the heart and then to the lungs. Then we breathe it out.

A drop of blood also has 10,000 white blood cells. White blood cells are the body's best way to fight off germs and infection. A drop of blood also has 250,000 platelets. Platelets help you to stop bleeding when you have been cut. Half of our blood is made up of gold-colored liquid called plasma.

# Experiment #4
# When Trouble Comes

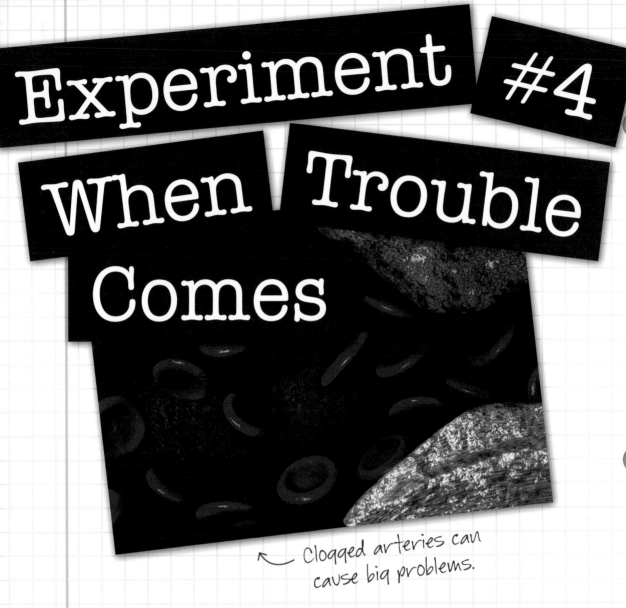

← Clogged arteries can cause big problems.

Just like any other system in the human body, the circulatory system can go wrong now and then. For example, arteries can sometimes become blocked. Remember, veins and arteries are just tubes. Over time, the walls of these tubes can get thicker. They can become lined with clumps of blood, old cells, or cholesterol. Cholesterol is a waxy substance that is made by the body and is found in many foods.

What do you think happens when arteries and veins get clogged? Let's form a hypothesis: **Fluids will move more slowly through blocked arteries and veins.** How can we test this?

**Here's what you'll need:**
- 3–6 drinking straws with different widths
- A bowl of plain yogurt
- A glass of water

You'll use straws instead of real blood vessels.

**Instructions:**
1. Stick the straw with the greatest width into the bowl of yogurt. It is not an easy way to eat yogurt, but it is possible. Suck the yogurt into the straw. Now, look at the straw. See how its sides are covered with yogurt?

2. Now, try to suck water through the same straw. What happens? Not much is able to come through, correct? It is the same with blood trying to get through a clogged artery. If you suck enough water through the straw, it can wash away the yogurt. Unfortunately, it is not the same with your arteries. Once they are clogged, it is almost impossible to get them unclogged without medication or surgery.

3. Try this experiment with the smaller straws. What happens as the width of the straws gets smaller and smaller?

Sucking yogurt through a straw is hard work!

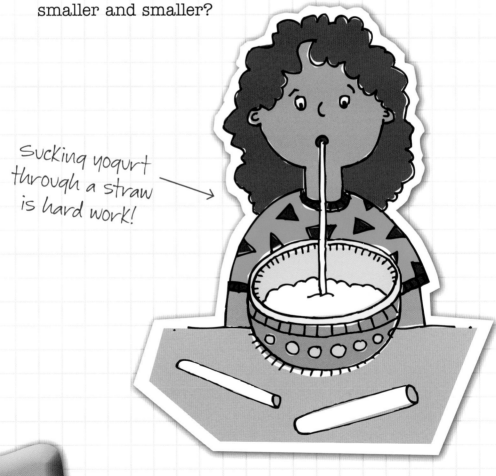

**Conclusion:**

What does this experiment tell you about your veins and arteries? What do you think occurs if blood is blocked or limited? Does this prove your hypothesis?

Your circulatory system is an amazing machine powered by a strong muscle that works night and day. It has thousands of miles of blood vessels that hold a lot of blood. The blood brings your body many of the things it needs to grow and stay healthy. Who knew all that was going on just under your skin?

How can doctors fix a clogged artery? One process is called an **angioplasty**. This is a type of surgery in which a doctor inserts a tiny balloon into the blocked blood vessel. Once it is in place, the doctor inflates the balloon with fluid. This flattens out the cholesterol, making room for the blood to flow. It is not unusual for the surgeon to then put a little tube, or stent, inside the blood vessel to keep it open.

# Experiment #5
# Tricks of the Trade

Earth's gravity pulls everything toward its surface, including your blood. Have you ever noticed the tingly feeling you get if you hold your arm in the air for too long? That is the feeling of blood draining out of your arm. What do you think happens to the color of your hand when the blood drains away?

You're working against gravity when you raise your hand.

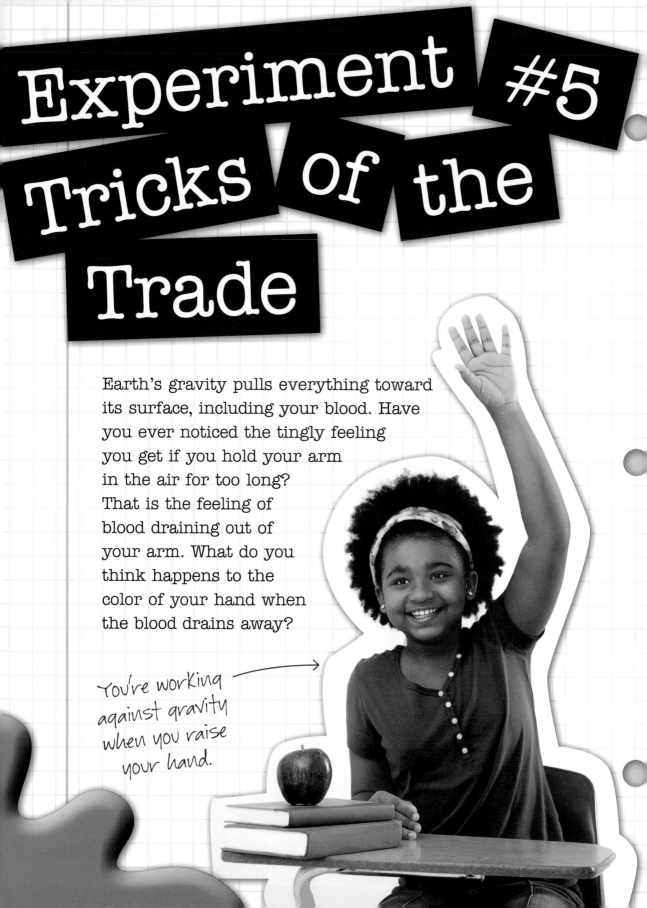

Let's come up with a hypothesis: **Your hand will get paler as blood drains from it.** We can test this hypothesis by performing a fun magic trick.

**Here's what you'll need:**
- A coin
- A friend

**Instructions:**
1. Place a coin on a table. Turn your back to your friend so you cannot see him or the coin.
2. Have your friend pick up the coin, but make sure you do not know which hand he is holding it in.
3. Have your friend hold the coin up to his forehead for 60 seconds.

4. When the time is up, tell your friend to hold out both of his hands. Both fists should be closed so that you cannot see which hand is holding the coin.
5. Turn around and look at your friend's hands. What do you notice about the two hands? Is one paler than the other? Which hand do you think is holding the coin?

**Conclusion:**

As your friend held the coin up to his forehead, the blood began to drain from his hand. With less blood in it, his hand became paler. This makes it easy for a magician—namely you—to see which hand he was holding the coin in.

How do you think skin color will affect your results? How could you experiment to find out?

Which hand do you think the coin is in?

# Experiment #6

## Do It Yourself!

Your circulatory system is at work all day long, every day. This means you can experiment with it at any time. Pay close attention to your heart rate as you do different activities. Take notes on how your circulatory system reacts to different events. For example, what happens to your heart rate when you watch a really scary movie? What about when you are just waking up in the morning?

If you keep track of different things your circulatory system reacts to, you will have an even better understanding of how it works. You can see that science is everywhere—even inside of you!

What kinds of experiments will you dream up?

# GLOSSARY

**angioplasty** (AN-jee-oh-plas-tee) a surgical procedure to repair a clogged artery

**capillaries** (KAP-uh-ler-eez) the smallest blood vessels in the body

**circulation** (sur-kyuh-LAY-shuhn) movement back and forth or around something

**circulatory system** (SUR-kyuh-luh-tor-ee SISS-tuhm) the system that moves blood from the heart to the rest of the body and back again through arteries, veins, and capillaries

**conclusion** (kuhn-KLOO-zhuhn) a final decision, thought, or opinion

**hypothesis** (hy-POTH-uh-sihss) a logical guess about what will happen in an experiment

**method** (METH-uhd) a way of doing something

**observations** (ob-zur-VAY-shuhnz) things that are seen or noticed with one's senses

**plasma** (PLAZ-muh) the liquid in blood that carries the cells

**platelets** (PLAYT-luhts) blood cells that help the body form clots and scabs

# FOR MORE INFORMATION

## BOOKS

Houghton, Gillian. *Blood: The Circulatory System*. New York: PowerKids Press, 2007.

Taylor-Butler, Christine. *The Circulatory System*. New York: Children's Press, 2008.

Whittemore, Susan. *The Circulatory System*. New York: Chelsea House Publications, 2008.

## WEB SITES

**KidsBiology.com—Human Biology**
www.kidsbiology.com/human_biology/index.php
Exciting pictures of the circulatory system in action

**KidsHealth—Your Heart & Circulatory System**
kidshealth.org/kid/htbw/heart.html
Facts about your heart and circulatory system

**The Yuckiest Site on the Internet—Your Gross and Cool Body**
yucky.discovery.com/flash/body/pg000131.html
Yucky factoids about the heart, veins, and blood

# INDEX

About the →
Author

Tamra Orr is the author of more than 200 nonfiction books for readers of all ages. She loves doing research. Orr lives in the Pacific Northwest with her husband, three teenagers, a cat, and a dog. She has a teaching degree from Ball State University and in her few minutes of spare time, she likes to write old-fashioned letters, read books, and look at the snowcapped mountains.